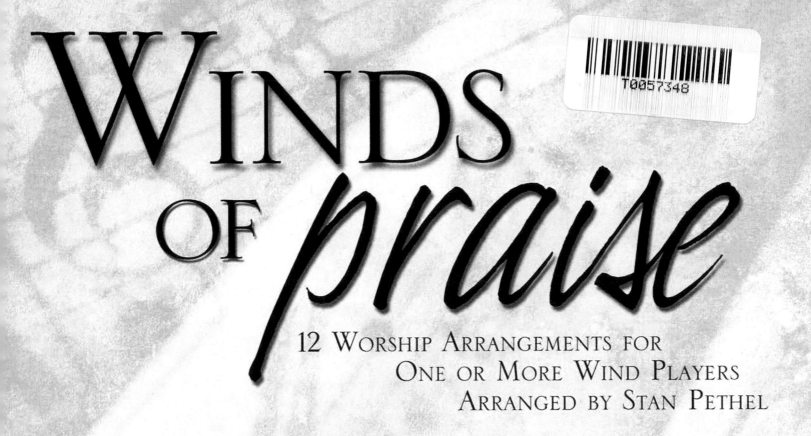

Winds OF praise

12 Worship Arrangements for One or More Wind Players
Arranged by Stan Pethel

Above All 30	In Christ Alone 15
As the Deer 24	Jesus, Draw Me Close 32
Come, Now Is the Time to Worship 4	Lord, I Lift Your Name on High 26
He Is Exalted 8	Sanctuary 18
Here I Am to Worship 12	Shine, Jesus, Shine 36
How Great Is Our God 21	You Are My All in All 34

PLAYBACK+
Speed • Pitch • Balance • Loop

To access audio, visit:
www.halleonard.com/mylibrary

Enter Code
4344-6695-5712-8079

ISBN 978-1-59235-205-0

SHAWNEE PRESS

EXCLUSIVELY DISTRIBUTED BY
HAL•LEONARD®

Visit Hal Leonard Online at
www.halleonard.com

World headquarters, contact:
Hal Leonard
7777 West Bluemound Road
Milwaukee, WI 53213
Email: info@halleonard.com

In Europe, contact:
Hal Leonard Europe Limited
42 Wigmore Street
Marylebone, London, W1U 2RY
Email: info@halleonardeurope.com

In Australia, contact:
Hal Leonard Australia Pty. Ltd.
4 Lentara Court
Cheltenham, Victoria, 3192 Australia
Email: info@halleonard.com.au

PREFACE

Winds of Praise was designed to allow for maximum flexibility of use. The uses range from full ensemble to solo instrument and piano. All of the arrangements will also work without piano. Just start at the first double bar or the pickups to the first double bar.

Here are some options:

1. Solo instrument and piano or track. The piano/score book works as accompaniment for all instruments as does the online audio accompaniment.

2. Multiple instruments and piano or track. Just have one instrument play the solo part and the other(s) the ensemble part along with the piano or online audio. Use more players on the solo part if needed to project the melody.

3. For instruments only, with no piano or audio accompaniment, these combinations will work:

   a. Brass Quartet – trumpet 1 & 2 with trombone 1 & 2 parts will stand alone. Start at the first double bar.

   b. Brass Quintet or Brass Sextet – For quintet use trumpet 1 & 2, horn, trombone 1, and tuba. For sextet add trombone 2. Start at the double bar.

   c. Other ensemble combinations. As long as trumpet 1 & 2 and trombone 1 & 2 are covered, the other parts will only add to the fullness of the ensemble. Piano adds even more and fills out the harmony. For instruments only start at the double bar, with piano starting at the beginning.

   d. Remember these instrumental substitutions. Violins and oboes can play or double the flute part. Clarinets can play or double the trumpet parts. Cellos, bassoons, and baritones can play the trombone part. Bass trombone players may want to try the tuba part as well. The tuba part can also be covered by a bass setting from an electric keyboard to add depth to the sound.

These arrangements are good lengths for preludes, offertories, and featured instrumental performance in both church services and church or school concerts. The level of difficulty ranges from 2 ½ to 3. Most are also in good vocal range should you choose to add choral or congregational singing at appropriate places. If you have a rhythm section of piano, guitar, bass, and drums, there are chord symbols provided with some basic drum suggestions in the piano score.

Best wishes with these arrangements in your area of musical ministry.

Stan Pethel

PUBLICATIONS AVAILABLE:

HL35025933   PIANO / SCORE

HL35025935   FLUTE / OBOE / VIOLIN

HL35025930   ALTO SAXOPHONE

HL35025936   TRUMPET / CLARINET

HL35025932   FRENCH HORN

HL35025934   TROMBONE / TUBA / CELLO

Come, Now Is the Time to Worship

Trumpet 1&2 (Clarinet)
Ensemble

Music by **BRIAN DOERKSEN**
Arranged by **STAN PETHEL**

Come, Now Is the Time to Worship

**Trumpet (Clarinet, Tenor Sax,
Baritone Treble Clef)
Solo**

Music by **BRIAN DOERKSEN**
Arranged by **STAN PETHEL**

He Is Exalted

Trumpet 1&2
(Clarinet)
Ensemble

Music by **TWILA PARIS**
Arranged by **STAN PETHEL**

He Is Exalted

**Trumpet
(Clarinet, Tenor Sax)
Solo**

Music by **TWILA PARIS**
Arranged by **STAN PETHEL**

Here I Am to Worship

Trumpet 1&2
(Clarinet)
Ensemble

Music by **TIM HUGHES**
Arranged by **STAN PETHEL**

Here I Am to Worship

Trumpet (Clarinet, Tenor Sax,
Baritone Treble Clef)
Solo

Music by **TIM HUGHES**
Arranged by **STAN PETHEL**

Trumpet
(Clarinet, Tenor Sax,
Baritone Treble Clef)
Solo

In Christ Alone

Music by **KEITH GETTY** and **STUART TOWNEND**
Arranged by **STAN PETHEL**

In Christ Alone

Trumpet 1&2
(Clarinet)
Ensemble

Music by **KEITH GETTY** *and* **STUART TOWNEND**
Arranged by **STAN PETHEL**

Sanctuary

Trumpet 1&2 (Clarinet)
Ensemble

Music by **JOHN W. THOMPSON**
and **RANDY SCRUGGS**
Arranged by **STAN PETHEL**

Sanctuary

Trumpet
(Clarinet, Tenor Sax,
Baritone Treble Clef)
Solo

Music by **JOHN W. THOMPSON**
and **RANDY SCRUGGS**
Arranged by **STAN PETHEL**

Trumpet
(Clarinet, Tenor Sax,
BaritoneTreble Clef)
Solo

How Great Is Our God

Music by **Chris Tomlin, Jesse Reeves,** *and* **Ed Cash**
Arranged by **STAN PETHEL**

How Great Is Our God

Trumpet 1&2
(Clarinet)
Ensemble

Music by **Chris Tomlin, Jesse Reeves,** *and* **Ed Cash**
Arranged by **STAN PETHEL**

As the Deer

Trumpet 1&2 (Clarinet)
Ensemble

Music by **MARTIN NYSTROM**
Arranged by **STAN PETHEL**

Trumpet
(Clarinet, Tenor Sax,
Baritone Treble Clef)
Solo

As the Deer

Music by **MARTIN NYSTROM**
Arranged by **STAN PETHEL**

Lord, I Lift Your Name on High

Trumpet 1&2 (Clarinet)
Ensemble

Music by **RICK POUNDS**
Arranged by **STAN PETHEL**

Lord, I Lift Your Name on High

Trumpet
(Clarinet, Tenor Sax,
Baritone Treble Clef)
Solo

Music by **RICK POUNDS**
Arranged by **STAN PETHEL**

Above All

Trumpet 1&2 (Clarinet)
Ensemble

Music by **LENNY LEBRANC** *and* **PAUL BALOCHE**
Arranged by **STAN PETHEL**

Trumpet
(Clarinet, Tenor Sax,
Baritone Treble Clef)
Solo

Above All

Music by **LENNY LEBRANC** *and* **PAUL BALOCHE**
Arranged by **STAN PETHEL**

Jesus, Draw Me Close

Trumpet 1&2 (Clarinet)
Ensemble

Music by **RICK FOUNDS**
Arranged by **STAN PETHEL**

Trumpet
(Clarinet, Tenor Sax,
Baritone Treble Clef)
Solo

Jesus, Draw Me Close

33

Music by **RICK FOUNDS**
Arranged by **STAN PETHEL**

You Are My All In All

Trumpet 1&2 (Clarinet)
Ensemble

Music by **DENNIS JERNIGAN**
Arranged by **STAN PETHEL**

Trumpet
(Clarinet, Tenor Sax,
Baritone Treble Clef)
Solo

You Are My All In All

Music by **DENNIS JERNIGAN**
Arranged by **STAN PETHEL**

With an underlying beat (♩ = *ca. 72*)

Shine, Jesus, Shine

Trumpet 1&2 (Clarinet)
Ensemble

Music by **GRAHAM KENDRICK**
Arranged by **STAN PETHEL**

Shine, Jesus, Shine

**Trumpet
(Clarinet, Tenor Sax,
Baritone Treble Clef)
Solo**

Music by **GRAHAM KENDRICK**
Arranged by **STAN PETHEL**